To Barb
  & Mike

Éloïse

LETTERS TO A LOST CHILD

To people who how
precious life is,

Ghelandlee
Juillet 2002

Éloïse

LETTERS TO A LOST CHILD

Loïse Lavallée
translated by Christopher Stone

INSOMNIAC PRESS

Edited by Mike O'Connor
Designed by Mike O'Connor

National Library of Canada Cataloguing in Publication Data

Lavallée, Loïse
Éloïse : letters to a lost child

Translation of: Éloïse, poste restante.

ISBN 1-894663-23-3

1. Lavallée, Éloïse 2. Lavallée, Loïse 3. Children--Death--Psychological aspects. 4. Mothers and daughters. I. Stone, Christopher, 1948- II. Title.

BF789.D4L3713 2002   155.9'37   C2002-900742-9

The publisher gratefully acknowledges the support of the Canada Council, the Ontario Arts Council and the Department of Canadian Heritage through the Book Publishing Industry Development Program.

Printed and bound in Canada

Insomniac Press,
192 Spadina Avenue, Suite 403,
Toronto, Ontario, Canada, M5T 2C2
www.insomniacpress.com

THE CANADA COUNCIL | LE CONSEIL DES ARTS
FOR THE ARTS | DU CANADA
SINCE 1957 | DEPUIS 1957

ONTARIO ARTS COUNCIL
CONSEIL DES ARTS DE L'ONTARIO

This book was written and translated by the parents of a severely hurt child, Éloïse, who died after thirteen years of love, tenderness, pain and suffering. Another such child, Tracy Latimer, lead a parallel life to Éloïse. She died on the eve of her thirteenth birthday, but at the hand of her father, Robert, who could no longer witness or share her pain. For his compassion and courage, he now faces a life in prison with no eligibility for parole for ten years.

As parents to Éloïse, we mourned her well and fully. Robert and Laura Latimer could not mourn Tracy well and fully—the tendrils of an imbalanced judicial system seized hold and have harassed them since the morning of Tracy's death.

This book is for them.

We long ago stopped asking why;
to do so led to certain madness.
The who and when and what
sank quickly into bland irrelevance.
What might have been was the hardest;
evidence was before us daily in glimpses
of her beauty, strength and light,
of what was Éloïse herself.

> — your father

Éloïse, we learned much from you about working together in an alliance of support. You also taught us even more about courage and suffering. I dare hope that your passage has made me a better doctor and all of us who knew you, better people. You will stay with me and with others here as the little girl on the swing.

The little girl on the swing,
who, on a magnificent fall day,
like a wounded bird needing a short rest,
swayed with gentle movement in all her beauty,
and leaving her body,
slowly took flight, and ever so softly,
left us.

— your doctor

$\mathcal{S}$itting alone in your room, I have long dreaded this moment, seeking the right words, gentle words of love which will bring about your rebirth. Dizzy before this quest for missing words and with the need to come to terms with our new reality, I have arrived after opening and closing many doors. I have this constant, fine pain, a small needle piercing just above my heart; emptiness and pain mingled with doubt and panic. How can I recreate your beauty, your softness, your strength, your suffering, and above all, your magic? Faced with the task, I doodle, I let myself be distracted and wander so that I can hold back, just a little.

First I come to a picture of you at five months old. You are intact, smiling, with your brilliant cheeks and mirthful eyes, my little girl, so full of life. Just beside it is another image of you, ten years later at the pavilion, with your freckles showing springtime and your dainty straw hat slightly tilted to one side, cruelly emphasizing your too-open mouth. Two unknown adult hands try to hold your head in a natural position, while your eyes, blind to the world around you, seem to look inward with astonishment at your incomprehensible fate.

All your light, imprisoned.

On my right, a Rodin reproduction of a mother with her dying daughter, so soothing, the two of them forever fixed in a huge block of stone. Tenderness and pain chisled into rock. Warm with memory, I ponder the abandon of the girl in the ever-so-accommodating arms of her mother. Mother and child united across the divide between life and death, joined together in an indestructible union. With longing I witness the sharing of unconditional love and absolute endurance in an immutable present.

The image fades and I turn toward the door and a holiday photo taken a year after the accident. A warm smile moves in me as I see the meeting of father and daughter at the seaside, a majestic recognition of confidence and sharing. I also see the strength of the father's loyalty, he's ready to take on any-thing—what has already happened and what is to come.

Below, on the dresser, a kaleidoscope crafted by your doc-tor to assemble pieces of your life and death in its shining lenses—strands of hair, bits of ribbon—your memento mori. Seated silently in the corner, your doll is lost and out of place in your absence. On the wall, my large quilt made from your ribbons, barrettes and tinsel, feverishly sewn stitch by stitch in my mad hope to keep your presence with me and to survive your absence, reflects a little of you in its colors and textures. Quietly, I try in vain to capture your scent. It has already gone even from your slipper, limp without the contour of your lit-tle foot. I move about and try to feel your presence around me without success. The aching need to hold you in my arms dis-tracts me from everything else. Alone, I put my head down and resolve to start my desperate quest for reunion. Slowly, as if swimming upstream, I will join with you and once again feel your lightness in me.

Dearest little one,

I recall so clearly your birth on that radiant autumn day. I recall the very instant you slid away from me—your upraised fist, your tiny, intense face—ready for battle. I wonder if you already knew what was waiting for you, even before your first breath? Did you already know how hard it would be later to repeat this first primal urge, simply to breathe? Did you already know that you would war against stupidity, negligence and even the well-meaning goodwill of our society? And most of all, did you know you would have to struggle against the gravity of your state, against the very weight of your own body, which would slowly and relentlessly close in and smother you?

Whatever you were to become, dear one, your entry into this world was of spectacular beauty. Within moments, you resolutely took your place on life's side and with your first breath, inhaled liberty, love and commitment.

After your first seven months, you could hardly be blamed for feeling that destiny was smiling on you. You grew in harmony; you drank of my milk with such intensity that you made me look away; you took on the strength of a great migrant bird, but one that soon would be caged. Your strength, of such force that I still want to cry when I think of it, rooted you so well on the side of life with all its loves and struggles.

It is warm for the season. A blinding clarity makes every-thing shine. Three pairs of hands: mine and Nicolas' left on the smooth handle of the stroller, while deep in his right pocket he care-fully squeezes his ice-cream money. Éloïse's two hands are dancing like butterflies.

Is it possible, Éloïse, that on a springtime afternoon life can change so quickly?

Both of you, my new children, hardly contained by your soft skins, your cascading laughter and your imperious needs, surely it is you who have given me life. Your brother, the blond one, is on my right, already keeping up with my pace, so gifted with good nature and joy that he invites a loving smile and makes me radiant. And you, my little one, I push you along in front of me, unknowingly pushing you toward your fate. You were wearing your pretty May-blue bonnet, a promise of good fortune, and bearing happiness in your irresistible smile and the quiet strength of your body. With what confidence you abandon yourself to me, neither of us realizing I am guiding you to a terrible destiny. Soon, with a change of fortune as swift as a slap, within seconds, we will pass forever into another life.

There is only one street to cross, in full sunlight, in the middle of the day; one street, near deserted and too silent, as before a storm. Suddenly, out of nowhere, a car at full speed smashes everything. One scream in the blinding light. Then from the warm asphalt I pick up the pieces of your broken body, my broken life; dreams, fantasies of motherhood and the quiet joy of your brother, broken. Your father, who waited out this scene in the wings has just lost the serenity of family life forever. As in an unending nightmare, I see myself shocked and unbelieving, taking you in my arms. Desperately, I want to roll back the last moments that have changed everything we were; I seek to alter these last two minutes. Oh, dear God, only these last two minutes! The blade of time slices only once—merciless, irreversible.

I hold you in my arms.

Your rosy cheeks are the color of ashes.

Yet another photo of her in the body cast covering her from head to toe, even tucked in under her chin to immobilize her fractured leg and neck. Only her arms are free, miraculously mobile. Her lively, bright eyes look demurely from their corners, smiling, while two dimples on either side of her mouth belt out with laughter.

Shaken to the core of your being, you come back from destiny's first assault. There is a reprieve; a timorous hope prevails. You surface slowly with the determination that will become your trademark. Insistent life returns to you. You embark forcefully on the road to healing while your smile remains as wonderful as ever.

Then the night of 7 July 1978 is before us, an ugly reversal of fate. A somber night in a too-hot summer when they decided to remove your cast under a general anaesthetic, a dark night when the medical profession made sure you would be locked up in yourself forever.

The doctors say they don't understand what has happened; they avoid truthful answers and avoid looking at us when they interpret reality. They agree to speak of a severe anoxic insult, with inescapable consequences to the brain: severe spastic quadriplegia, cortical blindness, an unknown degree of general retardation and daily uncontrollable epileptic seizures.

We know too well what this verdict means. From a free being of unlimited potential, you have become this irreversibly hurt child, imprisoned to the end by the lethal, shrunken bonds of your body.

You have been buried alive.

Herself a blind, mute paralytic,
needing all our care
for feeding, changing, moving, seeing,
demanding, in imperious silence,
a never-ending roster of chores.

— your father

Dear one, it was little by little that we had to see you go, but each step was like piercing blows on the walls of hope. Each week brought its own pessimism. Each week a repetition of unsupportable grief:

the loss of your sight

of your speech

of your movement

finally, the loss of your brilliant intelligence.

It is at this moment that your true battle begins, the one you will win even in your defeat. All your being will be concentrated into a beacon of life energy—an emanating radiance that can only be described as a concentrated expression of love—and through this medium you will communicate with all those who come near you. For thirteen years, you will create a network of love and devotion wherever you go. You will be the single source of many alliances against adversity and of magnificent shared tenderness. We will witness your determination to live and we will come to know values which before you were unknown to us.

You will give our lives a unique meaning.

Life has quality when there is a capacity to love and be loved. You, my daughter, had a life of great quality. But we know you paid dearly for it. As the years wore on, each day became heavier, more painful, often cruel for you and for those of us who lived in such intense symbiosis with you.

Her swing chair, empty, drifts with the wind. So often we visited it with her for our evening coffee or to hear the morning birdsong. So many delicious moments, glued to one another. And in a declining October sunshine, a few hours before her death, her breathing close to snuffed out, her father and I swing with her for the very last time.

Éloïse, you died on the eve of your thirteenth birthday, in the same radiant autumn sunshine into which you were born, in the exhausted arms of your parents, who could no longer see you suffer. You left this world quietly, with a softness of which only you were capable; an intense tenderness, almost palpable, like velvet. As soon as you left, I knew that you lingered, hesitant and uncertain about crossing the barrier that would put you forever on the other side of the thick, mute window of death. My forehead pressed against the glass, my incredulous eyes alert, I tried for a long time to follow you from afar. You spread into the immensity with such force that we were left profoundly diminished.

The idea that I could somehow stay with you and watch over you did not come to me then; it was only later that I gave it some thought. But by then I didn't have the courage. Could my love for you have been less than I believed? I shrank away, I let my own needs take over. Perhaps I came to understand that during your long preparation for death, in your discrete and efficient way, you signaled your readiness to undertake the voyage alone and lovingly absolved your mother from having to follow.

I occasionally return to the same window and again try to glimpse you from afar. I sometimes even want to go after you, cross the same, mute pane and run in the clouds alongside you. You were so long a prisoner to your body and to my arms that it is strange to think of you as completely free. But now, from the depth of my desolation, I can only see you in movement. I imagine you laughing as you skip from planet to planet, and if I listen carefully, I can almost hear you singing with your head high, your luscious curls floating on the wind of eternity and your freckles like shooting stars.

I suppose that for now my cosmic reunion fantasy will remain only that. But who knows? And since I cannot rid myself of this current dimension, nor my pain, nor my longing for you, I have decided to put words end on end to make a golden string of words, stretched out across the abyss that separates us.

I shall send my letters general delivery to be sure that you will receive them.

Who knows, perhaps someday I may get a hint of a reply?

When one loses ones parents, one becomes an orphan. When one loses a spouse, one becomes a widow or widower. Curiously, there exists no word in the French [or English] *language to designate parents who lose a child, and this is symptomatic of the veil of silence and solitude that falls over them when they experience this tragedy.*

— Annick Ernoult-Delcourt, *Apprivoiser l'absence*

The Determination of Chickadees

*É*loïse,

On this first gray, cold, shivering autumn, your death has swept everything else away. On the surface, life has returned to its normal course and days take on their somber rhythm without embellishment. I am very obedient. I do as I should. I follow the steps well: right place, correct time. But the wheel of days turns in emptiness and everything I do is without sense or purpose. Surely someone has noticed the slight bow in my back or my eyes overflowing with tears at any time. To be honest, I know people are watching over me. Their discrete presences accompany me from afar so as not to jostle me further and yet, at the slightest sign of distress, they are with me, listening in silence, holding out their hands.

I really don't know if I cry for you or out of self-pity. I tell myself over and over that you had to leave me—of that I remain convinced. As a family we could no longer tolerate seeing you slowly fade away from us, suffering; our hopes and energies were at their lowest ebb. How much further could I have gone without sinking with you? You, too, had exhausted all avenues; you held on with the last thread of your strength; you stayed with us for as long as you could.

Then for you, as for us, time ran out.

You went because you could do nothing else. But in the wake of your departure, everything went with you, leaving behind a gaping, devouring hole.

I had always thought that once you were gone, I would still feel your presence very near, hovering over my right shoulder; that somehow in your own way you would accompany me as we continued our journey—one visible, the other not. But when I quickly turn and look around, when I close my eyes and listen carefully, there is nothing.

Éloïse?

Where are you?

How I miss your firm round cheek that I kissed with such appetite, the vanilla smell of your silky hair, so beautiful that you resisted any combing.

I miss your too-skinny, suffering body that wrapped around mine so well.

I have lost my television-watching buddy. Our bath is far too big for me alone. I can no longer behold a sleeping child.

Gone with you is my maternity, my deepest sense of purpose and responsibility. The center of the universe which tilted to you at your birth has now swung back empty into my arms and I can't deal with it. All is to be rebuilt from a new starting point, and my life, though I value it passionately, is but suffering, with its raison d'être now amputated.

Sitting under the bright Christmas tree with her feet on Brandy, who jealously guards her, she seems happy. The lights shine in her eyes. Nicolas tries to guess what is hidden in his presents and the fever of preparation gives every little gesture a festive air.

Happiness chooses it's own time.

Winter has sealed us in its white envelope and the house is quiet as never before—cruelly empty. Through the window overlooking the bird feeders, I watch the gently falling snow. A violent urge to live wells up in me as I watch the peacefulness outside my window. Three cardinal couples flame their magic reds and browns against an unending whiteness, while the frenetic and determined chickadees try to convince me that life continues. They are right. Through them, it is as though you had sent me a clear sign, forcefully urging me forward. But what direction should I take first?

Your wonderful wisdom always expressed itself in this same determination: to live fully in the present; to be what you could be despite everything that limited you; to enrich us with your presence, and to receive in return, with such easy acquiescence, our unique love for you. Now it is my turn to experience the present and give full rein to today.

My uneasiness continues at the thought of having abandoned you when you needed me most to accompany you in the last step of your life. I helped you live and helped you die. But Éloïse, my sweet child, please forgive me, I can go no further, I cannot leave with you. I must say no.

The go here for this (a simple chair)
The go there for that (a pillow)
The automatic doors
The ramps (and those that weren't)
The waiting in waiting waiting rooms
The close-to-hostile stares
The well-meaning, uncomfortable smiles
And, most cruel, the helpless paralysis of friends

— your father

I've just returned from a long walk to the cemetery. The sky was so blue, the snow so brilliant, the undercurrent in the air so mild that flowers actually grew on your grave through the snow. Mauve on white—your colors. I lay down on the snow angel I made the day before, I let the warmth of the February sun penetrate me, and as I closed my eyes, I felt the earth vibrate under me.

I remind myself—four months already.

The mirror reflects my image superimposed on yours
Hair that curls in the humidity
Lively freckles
The stubborn rosette at our widow's peak
The sly, sideways smile
The color of our eyes
The unquenchable thirst of our search

We looked so much alike (you being even more beautiful, as your father would tenderly say) it was as if we were a single person in two different bodies. When we decided to call you Éloïse I was fearful that only one of us could survive with such similar given names: Éloïse and Loïse. Secretly, I believed it was I who would disappear. Parents go first, that's the natural order of things. Then as I watched you suckle with eagerness, you stared into my eyes with such insistence that I had to look away. I was often discomforted by so intense an exchange. As years went by, I would try very hard to put myself in your place—I wanted to know better what would please you, what hurt you. In return, you listened so intently to my slightest complaints, to my sweet nothings and my chats, that we each became a mirror for the other. The unbearable difference was that I watched this other me wither and perish.

Now that you have gone, I can finally rest from having to carry you, but it is as though I have been bombed out: I'm an empty desert, impossible to repopulate.

Now in the southwest of my heart there will always be a great cemetery, a no man's land, where no flower will ever bloom.

First Dream

We're in the kitchen. Without success, your father tries to feed you. It is one of those usual Saturday mornings when he takes over. He patiently brings the spoon to your mouth and back again several times. Exasperated, he finally calls me to come and asks for my help. I tell him it is impossible, that you can't eat because you are dead. He insists that I try. So I take the spoon and begin to feed you. Your mouth doesn't open and the food flows down your cheeks. We both realize that you really are dead and feeding you is hopeless.

I awake in infinite sadness.

It's late and I can't sleep. The night is full of familiar nois-es: furnace, radiators, hot water pipes, fridge, creakings. It is the time for fantasies, anguish and exultation. These are the hours when the imagination runs like wild horses, when the heart beats in a body so aware of itself. It is also a time when the rooms of the soul open up one by one, banging open their doors; when the windows of desire give onto infinite possibil-ity. Only when everything sleeps peacefully can my delirious-ness and wildness rise—there is no one to bring them into line.

I want to go barefoot in the snow. I want to breathe in the cold, dry February air. The door opens on a mysterious space and I go forward into the icy snow, my heart full of desire. Shivers race up my spine as I start to run, alone and laughing, in the cutting cold under an astonished moon. Breathless, I let myself fall into the inviting nothingness and for a brief second I want to make this moment last forever. Oh, these marvelous suspended moments when I wish that time would stop!

I come back inside, dry off and wrap myself in blankets. I go into your room and lock the door. I write notes, poems, let-ters, crazy words, calls for help, hymns of ecstasy. I write because it is impossible for me to remain still in this turmoil of contradictory emotions, because without this frantic writ-ing I would be reduced to never-ending tears.

Finally, I begin reading my diary and go back in time to June 23, 1978, just after the accident but before your irrevoca-ble brain damage. I find this entry:

Éloïse must stay in her cast another four weeks. She cried a lot in the hospital today when they tried to make changes to her chin piece. Her body is now all locked in; only her arms are free, moving like busy butterflies. She was so happy to ride in the car and come back home afterward. Tonight my body is aching as though I have been beaten. I'm physically exhausted—Éloïse is very heavy to carry with all her plaster—and morally exhausted from seeing her so hurt and from putting so much hope in her healing. Another weekend in front of us, the four of us together, to love and fight so that she heals quickly.

~&

Had the thought of you not healing already taken hold in me? Had I conceived that this fight would be drawn out over the next thirteen years? I'm not sure, for if this terror sometimes surfaced, I surely pushed it away from me with all my might. I am certain of one thing: these thirteen years have seen tiny hope and great discouragement, unlimited energy and unconditional love, an unending roster of chores, care and wearing down.

Tonight I feel terminally worn down by each one of those years. Once more awash with tears, I take you up in my arms and put you away in one of my interior rooms; a special place where there is still music and sunshine. I want to keep you with me. I don't want to let you go—it's out of the question—and so, without making a sound to frighten you, I close the door and turn the lock. Whether you like it or not, you will remain with me now and follow me wherever I go.

There, my child. Now that I know you are not completely gone, I breathe more easily. Unseen, I take a glimpse behind the other doors of my soul and meet those few people I love so dearly. Far from distancing them from me, your death has made me love them more. The living offer themselves to me, they lead me by the hand and populate my journey.

But there is still life. Life to drink in great mouthfuls, spilling down my chin and neck; life fused in every budding flower, in every growing relationship, pushing my limits of new frontiers further and further.

Dearest one,

My arms ache for you. Having taken care of a child like you for such a long time, there is a carefully defined space between my left arm, where your head lay, and my right arm, which held your legs. Now there is emptiness in that space, so heavy, Éloïse.

No one, you hear, no other child, husband, lover or friend could ever put themselves in that space.

My arms are as tense and spastic as yours were and there are days when they open only to the memory of you.

During the unending month of March—her exhausted, hurt body, her labored breathing—the doctor stoops over her, listening to her chest. I am convinced that it is the end, but he tells me the time has not yet come.

What more does he need?

How can I, her mother, not know the worst?

With calming tones, he assures me that the moment is not now—he will know and he will tell me when it comes. And he will keep his word. But when he does, nearly two years later, I will not be able to believe him, and on that very morning, I will go to work as though nothing could happen, as though I had understood nothing.

Because I no longer want, no longer wish, for her to leave me.

Today is the beginning of March. Do you remember how March was always your worst month? In a way, I am glad that you don't have to negotiate springtime once again. I remember that last March, how you had already decided that you had had enough, that you would not continue to live as you were. It took eight more months for you to decide definitively, and for us, your parents, to accept that it was time for you to leave us. Even though you died in October, it was in that same springtime that you started to slowly disappear. You know, I sometimes still believe the telephone will ring and it will be the hospital telling us that it is time to come and get you, that you are ready to come home to us. Oh, how I would like to go and get you! But at the same time I don't want you coming back to us as you were—ruined, diminished, in such pain.

We couldn't stand it any longer.

Accepting the reality of the wheelchair took a long time. We used all possible substitutes to avoid the issue: special chairs, invented strollers, cushions, beanbags, hammocks, swings. But above all we used our arms: arms that carried her everywhere, arms that sheltered her while she was fed, that held her so close to our hearts.

Finally, despite efforts to camouflage it, the chair remained ugly, shocking, ungracious.

My guilt is over. The day we put you into the earth I laid this huge weight alongside you.

Guilt for the first wrong step, the worst ever taken. It was with your mother, crossing the street on a sunny Sunday, in your blue hat, eyes shining with confidence, that your life was so suddenly overturned. The precise instant when the balance tilted to suffering, when innocence floated away like a bubble, burst in the sun and was gone forever.

Several weeks afterward, I was leaving the hospital on the arm of your grandfather, guilt with the deep blue sky of a warm July evening while you were lying in the air conditioned reaches of intensive care. My first bath after the accident was so warm and good, yet all the while I was thinking of you, tied down, punctured, plastered, intubated—oh, dearest one, so cold.

In the days and weeks, the months and years that followed, every moment of my pleasure became a spring of guilt.

Guilty of a stroll at the end of the day while you could never walk.

Guilty of all the autumn colors, the flowers, the beloved faces that you would never be able to caress with your own eyes.

Guilty of breathing crisp November air, while for hours and hours you labored with each rasping, concentrated breath.

Guilty of lovemaking, while you, my beloved, would never know the serene joys of womanhood.

Guilty of leaving when we went on a trip. Each time we left, nothing could make me leave behind this feeling of weakness, knowing we were leaving without you, seeking pleasure as a family while excluding you. No baggage was as heavy to carry as knowing you were elsewhere, and the trip home always lightened this load as it brought me closer to you.

Guilty of sleep when you were sick in the next room, having to close your door so as not to hear your desperate breathing.

Guilty of the beauty of my own body beside your scoliosis, your dislocated hip, your swollen gums, your deformed spasticity and your pretty mouth, ungraciously held open by gravity.

Guilty, finally, of remaining alive and of your ultimate abandonment.

Guilty of life.

Éloïse, I admitted my guilt for all these years. My sentence is pain, emptiness, exile and aloneness. Listen to me carefully now, I want you to be the first to know: I have exhausted every twist of guilt. I am finished with it. I now want to live without ever having to excuse myself for feeling well. You understand, never! I will try to do as little harm as possible, but I swear to you that when life extends its hand to me I will no longer look aside. You know very well, don't you, that at this point in my life I can no longer sin by omission, that I want to expand to every frontier, that I have decided to fulfill my desires, my hopes and all the choices that will flow from them.

I believe to do anything else would be destructive.

It is impossible to be abstract about her absolute physical dependency; for everything.

However, the tortured road that she followed is hers, alone.

The strange interior blossom that produced her special aura is hers, alone.

The strength in sweetness and will to live remain the prerogative of her realm, alone.

Last summer, during your last months, your father, who always gave you teasing nicknames, found a new one. Home from work, he would give you a big hug and greet you as "Saddam Hussein." For him, you were a great terrorist. You held us all hostage. He was not far off, because you held us hostage better than anyone could. I am sure that you, even as hurt as you were, knew very well your power over us. You who knew better than I the depth of my love and devotion. To hold you tightly in my arms, to kiss you, to whisper softly to you, to sing of my need for you. How could we be reproached for enjoying these mutual, gratifying pleasures?

Sick and in pain, you were so content whenever we shared in your suffering. Your grandmothers and I became experts. You made sounds which amplified your frustration, our laments replied in cadence. With you we created a song of such sadness, yet a song which consoled us all.

The Second Dream

We're in your room. Your father is putting together your crib. I tell him it's useless because you are dead. He gets angry and says you're not dead, but you're right there on the mattress under the baby sheet. I reply that it can't be you, it is just a doll that looks like you. He insists I do something because you are crying. I realize the doll is crying; I pick it up gently and it stops. You have become this doll. You breathe, you look deep into my eyes, and fully aware, in peace, you die content in my arms.

I awake and close my arms around infinite emptiness.

Six months into my pregnancy your eyes were not only well formed, but opened, and you could make a fist—ready for the fight. I had already gained fourteen pounds, and during a visit with the doctor I was astonished to hear the rapid patter of your heart. In the twilight of a hot June day, after working in the garden, I clearly remember lying down naked on my bed with a pre-eminent tummy, red from the sun, feeling you roll around amusing yourself. I felt your movement, I talked to you in silence—we were already so attuned to each other.

Six months after your birth, I had already stopped breast-feeding. Looking back, I now think I found it very difficult to deal with your intense gaze. At that early stage you were crawling everywhere. With your four new teeth you were a show-stopper and enjoyed every moment of it.

Yet I was anxious.

As I watched both you and Nicolas, I worried about the fragility of this state of grace, the perfect balance that only an atmosphere peopled by happy, healthy children can produce. It was as though I had sensed what was being prepared for us, of what would happen in the months to come.

Six months after your accident you were in and out of hospital so many times. You put all your energy into telling us that you wanted to stay with us, to stay alive. As for us, we often thought that you might be better off dead. But it was never said out loud. More than once we were tempted: pneumonia without antibiotics, refusal of a catheter, unadjusted anticonvulsant medication. But from within your prison it was you, Éloïse, who decided you wanted to continue, and we accepted your decision, allowing you to stay on this side of life.

Six months after your death, I often go to the cemetery

and walk around your ashes in a sort of sad waltz. I so much want you to come and warm me.

Yes, I know. I know I must let you get further from me for your good as well as mine, but I can't—I am as stubborn and hard-headed as my embraces are soft.

All those deathly hours waiting in hospital rooms.
Waiting in the corridors of worry and suffering.
Waiting for the appearance of a doctor for the dreaded confirmation of a prognosis.
Waiting.
And above all, not wanting to hear
what they didn't want to tell us.

I am tired. I still resist. As strongly as I can. Can you tell me where I can find rest when everything slides around me, when reality is fluid, ungraspable, when my own emptiness makes me dizzy?

I want neither to understand nor accept. My anger is insistent. I drum my hand on the tight skin of my pain in search of a magic incantation.

I am tired, but the ever-turning continues in me, by the bird fields or in the star fields, in search of your planet. Will ever I meet you one day, one night, in the meadow's wild grasses or in a comet's vapor?

I want neither to understand nor accept. My anger is insistent. I drum my hand on the tight skin of my pain in search of a magic incantation.

I am so tired, but I am determined to take up again those empty, ordinary tasks that have lost all power to soothe. I know you're neither in your swing chair, nor under a tree in the cemetery. I know you're neither in the little slipper I hug so close to my heart, nor in your ribbons I put in my hair.

I want neither to understand nor accept. My anger is insistent. I drum my hand on the tight skin of my pain in search of a magic incantation.

I could be content by looking for you inside myself. But that is not enough! Just as it is not enough for me to see the light of love reflected in the eyes of those who knew you. It seems that nothing will ever be enough.

I want more, much more.

Éloïse, please tell me why I am putting so much energy into seeking you where you are not?

Please, answer me...

In my head, my heart, my arms,
on mountains, rivers, prairies,
on busy days and sleepless nights,
while rambling in fallow fields
or simply turning the earth...

The echo of absence, the purgatory of tears.

Her father liked to lift her up in one long body stretch. Spastic and unwilling to extend, her arms would open out as in an offering.

Then she would smile at him.

And I would take her hands, her long, stiff fingers, and run them over my face, softly placing them on my mouth and there firmly say: Mama.

Then to her face, caressing with the back of her hand her opened mouth and murmur: Éloïse.

Then we would kiss.

It is near midnight and because I can't sleep, I decide to join you at the cemetery. I rest against the gravestone next to yours. The name Benedict is cut into the stone. I consider the impenetrable dark silence in a desolate landscape. Even though the fireflies rhythmically light up around me, I really can't see what I'm writing. There are no mosquitoes, the stars above are arranged wildly and the leaves form a somber yet comforting lace against the sky.

I try not to cry, but without success. Incorrigible, I say to myself that you, too, would probably want to cry but that isn't done where you are. Stubbornly I wait and wait for you, my soul shriveling and in pain. I am here, I'm giving myself to you, don't you see me? Oh, how much I want you. For just a moment come and put your head against my shoulder so that I can again smell the sweetness of your hair and hold your soft fragile neck in my hands.

I close my eyes, trying to sleep on the grass, my head on your marker. It is so very hard. Maybe I will come back later and spend a whole night here with you. I am sure we would sleep well together.

In her room there were a dozen music boxes of all shapes, sizes and colors. Each one had its own music, often sad and repetitive, but on certain evenings there were great concerts. Just before lights out, her brother would set all the music boxes going at once. The dog would start howling, she would get so excited and Nicolas laughed through it all.

Today is my birthday. I would like it if you came and spoke to me. I would hug you to my heart and fill myself with your sweet presence. How could you know what a vortex I am turning in, my eyes blinded by a well of tears, my open arms spread powerless and lifeless, my hair blown this way and that by winds of sadness and despair.

How could you know there are days like yesterday, when I felt you resonating in my passions and raging fantasies, and then days like today, when I uselessly flap my wings?

How could you know I now wear your ribbons and barrettes as I rock in your chair at night, embracing your slipper, and that I now play the piano where I once lay watching you breathe?

How could you know that I manage my time to the minute lest I fade away? How vulnerable I am to this aching emptiness of not seeing you, not touching you, not breathing you in? How difficult it is for me to tame this new dimension of our intimacy? How often I must shake myself, scattering the dust of the past, and once more try to fill myself with resolve?

How could you know that, through you, I have become closer to the budding flowers, the soaring birds, the vital impulse of life? Did you know that the tenderness we shared has become an enveloping wave flowing from my heart out through my fingertips?

Did you know that it is to you that I owe my renewed sensuality, a renegotiated taste for life, an aired-out set of values?

Yes, I think you do know all this. And I thank you for being so patient with me, for waiting for me while I detour through despair, worry and anger. I thank you for imperceptibly accompanying me each day. I thank you for permitting this new understanding of myself, this other initiation to life, and above all, for departing before it was too late for either of us. Finally, I thank you for not leaving me completely, for you do know how difficult it would be to continue alone, without you.

Éloïse, can you hear me?

Mama,

On this first Mother's Day of our separation, I want you to know that you were, are and will always be, a very special mother...not unlike me as a daughter.

I would wish a mother such as you for every hurt child who has to live with what I lived with. Thank you, Mama, for letting go of me when it was time.

I want you to know that thanks to your sensitivity and sympathy, despite all the limitations, we built a wonderful intimacy with moments of intense sweetness.

I want you to know how much I regret your sleepless nights. I am still looking for a special timepiece that can adjust your sleep, put out of kilter forever by thirteen years of disquiet.

I want you to know you are my favorite gardener, and in getting closer to the earth, to flowers and their cycles, you are also getting closer to life.

I want you to know I miss the ribbons you put in my hair and that I have found nothing that can replace your warm embrace. In a way, your visits to the cemetery remind me of our peaceful, silent moments together. Thank you, Mama, for having kept me with you for so long. I am now free and you must no longer feel guilty for living without me.

I also want you to know that what may have appeared to you as manipulation was the only way to tell you yes, no, more, enough and thank you.

I want you to know that if I had become a woman and a mother, I would have wanted to be like you. Your faithfulness was my security, allowing me to go to bed at night happy, and finally, supporting me when I closed my eyes for the last time.

I want you to know that since that October afternoon I am one with eternity, in this uncharted and untamed land.

Mama, above all, I want you to know that you are still my mother, and I will love you forever.

The Mourning Dove Coos

With care I hand her to her father who puts her into the coffin. She is in her pyjamas, tucked in to her favorite blanket with her pink teddy. We each kiss her one last time. With my fingertips I softly touch her forehead.

The lid is closed.

Her body is leaving us.

Each nail drills into heartbreaking emptiness and sadness.

On a June evening the earth was warm and the polished marble of your urn was so smooth it felt soft to the touch. Your father felt that you had not been properly buried. We decided to reposition you, "straightening her up," in his words. It did us good to redo this ritual in the setting sun of the summer solstice, when the days are long enough to believe in eternity. I held you on my knees, your father prepared the earth, and all the while we were surrounded by memories of you. After a moment of silence we set your ashes at the bottom of a perfectly dug hole. One after the other, we caressed your urn, and for a second time, buried you.

This time, forever.

My dearest one,

Leaning against Benedict's stone, I hear the cooing of a mourning dove as summer-almost-here stretches lazily over the cemetery. A gibbous moon rivals a setting sun, the air's kiss is humid in these confines of death, and I am enlivened by heightened sensations that give me such a vivid sense of being alive and of this world, body and soul.

Freedom comes to me in easy breathing, being able to open wide my arms, flap my wings, soar the wind and glide with the rhythm of hope.

I am swept away by wonderment and acceptance, ready for the new cycles of life and all the experiences awaiting me.

I feel a great capacity to love, which has always been a source of happiness for me, enlarging, pushing my limits and carrying me to fabulous caprices.

And yet, I am in distress for all that has gone by me and will never be mine—unexplored absolutes, explosions of tenderness, losses of innocence.

I feel grateful for those moments of fragile and enchanting happiness, grateful for simple gestures reaching into infinity.

Everything here is so beautiful.

Summer has arrived quietly. I know that this season can be at once marvelous and intolerable. When the floodgates of nature burst open, when the breeze is too heavy with heat and the sun too hot, I fear the loss of my autonomy. It is as if the essence of my life is overflowing and could desert me forever.

Once again, it is time to leave. I smile and lift my eyes

to the sky. The great vault looks somber, but far out, brilliant and inviting, the moon rides majestically high above.

Beside the pool, under the maple, the hammock is seldom used now. We put Éloïse there on the too-hot days of summer, folding over her the white, light clouds of the mosquito netting.

She listened to our voices and those of the frogs, cicadas, crickets and birds.

She listened to summer.

I thought this July would bring me closer to you but your presence is ever more fleeting. The panic of emptiness and misery overtakes me. Your absence has become definitive, but I can't reconcile myself to your leaving. I decide to spend the night at the cemetery.

When I think of it now, I can't really say why. Did I honestly believe that I could find you? That you would come?

Against all logic and wisdom, I did it.

With a shrug of your father's shoulders and a worried look from your brother, I set out for the night, certain that something would happen at your grave. The night air was soft and the starry sky was clear. I must admit that I felt quite comfortable under the tree near your grave. I didn't seem out of place laying down amidst the gravestones. It felt very normal, natural. A few hours later, though, I was still staring dumbly into a sky full of stars, finding it empty and unreadable. Time passed slowly but nothing happened, undisturbed by a nap. With all the asleep-for-eternity around me one would think that they would have had some influence on me. Insomnia proved to be more exasperating than the mosquitoes. I began to feel absurd. I put on my shoes, packed up my sleeping bag and stomped home, angry with myself, with you, completely desperate and full of an impatient sadness.

I slipped into bed without disturbing your father who, the following morning, suggested I might sleep on the golf course the next night.

And I lay down on the redwood needles and seemed to flow the canyon with the thunder and confusion of the stream, in a happiness which, like birth, can afford to ignore the blood and the tearing. For nature has no time for mourning, absorbed by the turning world, and will no matter what devastation attacks her, fulfill in underground ritual, all her proper prophecy.

— Elizabeth Smart, *By Grand Central Station I Sat Down and Wept*

Out of the question, no vacation for me this summer; it's best to keep moving. I need the regimen of days, the structure and function of work—rise at the same hour, dress, put make-up on, do my job—all so that I can forget that my center has collapsed and I can't put it back together.

I no longer have the consolation of thinking about you. How could I go about it? In what context? In the fleeting memories of you that come and go in this ruined present? In the infinite that I can't grasp or understand? In my mind, in my heart, through all these objects that surrounded you but now mean nothing because you are dead?

I miss your presence and I can no longer rally myself around your spirit. Your memory clashes with the present. Your absence has become even more unbearable. So I busy myself, I use up restless energy through calculated, precise gestures and activities that keep me standing. I rarely sit, I sleep even less—I consider it a vocation to stay in motion.

The week has been long, hard and empty. It is now Friday and I need a friendly presence, a consoling ritual, some ambient tenderness. Alone in the car, I drive without a soothing thought. It is very hot, the road is beckoning, but I don't know where to go. Moving with gathering momentum, in my mind I see a field of yellow grasses, where the earth is dry and the hard sun beats wonderfully on my shoulders—I had almost forgotten that field. I remember a nest, ingeniously hidden in a shrub, with its treasure of red-winged blackbird eggs. Relieved to have found a new purpose, I seek out the field and find the nest in the middle of it. My heart beats faster, I am breathless; they've just hatched. Tiny chicks, downless, cry out, life blossoming from their open throats.

A long sigh is forced from me. In tears, I caress these tiny bodies, at once fragile and resistant, so much like yours. How

I would like to lie down in the grass, put them on top of my empty womb and watch them gambol there all afternoon. Out of respect for the parents, agitating about my head, I decide not to. Transfixed, I stay a long while observing them, watching their breathing, seeing them struggle in the disorder of birth and life.

Slowly I walk away, deeply breathing in the smell of the earth, and dally by the sentinel trees. All around me yellow flowers bob in the wind, fence posts lean askew and the irresistible smell of pine needles floats on the air.

Flooded by the beauty of this field, I bond once more to life, which reasserts itself in the magical and powerful cycle of nature. Life is holding out its hand to me and I shake it firmly.

I now know I will survive.

Third Dream

We're at home. Your father is looking for you everywhere. I tell him it is useless to continue, to stop looking because you are dead. He doesn't want to believe me and desperately goes from one room to another. Finally he returns to me with you in his arms. He is walking with difficulty, crying, and says that he can't go on. He asks me to take you. I am so happy that he has found you. He carefully gives way to me and I am immediately transfixed by the light in your eyes. Now secure in my arms you look deeply into me and die peacefully.

I wake with a heavy sadness, yet I feel the warmth of your presence.

Now, more than ever, I am aware that you are irrevocably gone and I find it hard to come to terms with this. I often feel as though I am huddled in a tight ball, waiting for the storm to pass. The wind is strong, the sun is blotted out, hail drops from the sky, and yet, moments later, drought sets in.

Then, gradually, the air softens. I hear birds, I lift my head, look around me and breathe freely for a few days. Then it begins again. I fold into myself more tightly and once more await the approaching storm.

You see, I have yet to know how to live with you, my dead daughter. Living and death contradict each other even though one is intimately a part of the other.

Éloïse, you are dead.

I think that I have just now truly understood. During your last spring and summer we watched you fade, wishing an end to your suffering. When your doctor told us it was the beginning of the end on that October Monday, I didn't really believe him.

My sweet child, I was sure you would rally as you always did. It was only on Wednesday afternoon, after your last morphine injection, I knew you were coming to the final break. In my arms, twenty minutes later, with a profound last sigh, your breathing slowly ran down to nothing, and you gave a shudder that shook my body. Yet, I still did not believe. In the months that followed, when I held onto you in different ways, I refused to look into the emptiness of this abandonment out of fear of slipping in.

I have tried to perpetuate you in life even though you left nine months ago. I can't do it any longer. A few weeks ago, when I held your ashes once again and rocked them gently, I understood how much I missed you and understood that this missing you would never end. We were so tied to each other that I am unprepared, unable to face this ultimate separation. So, as a reflex, I fold in on myself, roll up like a ball, and wait for the storm to pass. But the storm is always on the horizon, ready to strike.

We are both floating, fragile and naked, in the white foam of the bath, enveloped in the soft suds and warmth. Her father takes her out for the vigorous rub-down, the blue hair dryer, and her favorite above all, Mama's powder.

I am thinking of you again, holding on tight to the reins of my memory. Will I never let you rest? My arms burn with the many memories of your passage: your warmth, your softness, your fragility. They feel the heaviness of your head, the rigidity of your arms, the skinniness and coldness of your legs. It's all imprinted on them. My body has memories engraved into it from your intensity, your concentration on living and the love I could read in your eyes. And finally, the later memories are burned into me: memories of your suffering, your panic and our mutual fear of parting forever.

It was necessary to give her permission to die, to let her know that she could leave us for her great migration. I repeated to her several times that she could go. I know her father did as well. But because she was afraid, we also silently committed to be with her to the very end, to never leave her alone and to allow no one to touch her, after, except out of love.

Another sleepless night. I have tried everything. Because I couldn't find anything else to do, I got into Nicolas' empty bed with your pillow. The persistent crickets keep me company, I imagine myself the lone survivor on a deserted beach, without moon or stars, as I used to say to my little son. How beautiful was our chant of happiness:

— Why is your mama rich?
— Because we love each *other*!
— Love each other as big as what?
— As big as the *sky*!
— The sky without the moon?
— And without the *stars*!

And you, my dear one, what sky have you gone to? It seems as though you have moved further away. You see I didn't think that death would come by instalments, by degrees, and that it could take such an interminably long time. In this sleepless moment, I recall with nostalgia the night that followed your death, the peaceful night of keeping vigil with you.

When you left us at the end of that October afternoon we didn't wish to separate from you, and as promised, we kept you at home with us. Your father and I knew that this was not the very end, there remained one final small corridor to pass through silently, the three of us together, on tiptoes.

Those who needed to continued their vigil with you discreetly, each in their own way, and the first hours of your death went by with a simple intimacy, devoid of happiness but not yet full of suffering. It was true that we were alone, but in an insolent way you remained with us, physically accessible.

When night came, I moved you slightly to make room for me at your side. I was surprised to find that even seven hours after your death your bed was still warm from your spent fever. I lay down in this warmth and closed my eyes. I slept as I had not for years, as I have not since: peacefully, deeply, a healing sleep. My body unconsciously registered that it no longer had to watch over your fragile breathing, while my soul still had not felt the pain of missing you.

On reflection, you were probably not as completely dead as all that; you had probably just crossed the threshold of life and you were keeping me with you to the soft limits of death. True, you no longer breathed, and at last, suffered no more, but you were not yet so far away. Looking back, it seems that you were my guide for that night of sleep, and it was your authority, my sweet girl, that watched over your father and me.

Perhaps in the early morning, witnessing my awakening, you left just as I opened my eyes. I sat up to look at you, my dead little girl. The rigor had set into your expression but your aura was still there. Sadly then, I knew that your journey with us would soon be over.

Papa was asleep on the floor beside your bed. I knew that once he was awake we would have to continue our walk on the path to death. We were at a point of no return, we could tarry no longer, the three of us together in that fragile, peaceful union. I held on for a few more moments, suspended and attached to you. I looked at your gentle face as I had every morning before waking you for school. I caressed your hair and said good morning.

Then time caught up with me. The sun was rising and the first day of your death marked the dawn of the rest of my life.

Ma petite est comme l'eau,
Elle est comme l'eau vive.
Elle court comme un ruisseau
que les enfants poursuivent.

Courez, courez
vite si vous le pouvez.
Jamais, jamais,
Vous ne la rattraperez.

...Pleurez, pleurez,
si je demeure esseulée.
Le ruisselet
au large s'en est allée.

— *L'Eau Vive,* Guy Béart

The quilt of memories is finished. Many tiny stitches, one after the other, resolutely done to try to soften my loss, an attempt to prolong your presence through familiar things. Only after I have exhausted these rituals will I be able to explore other ways of taming myself. In touching the quilt with my fingertips, I remain with you a little. In furtive, precise flashes, memories come to me linked to its colors and textures—a swatch of your pyjamas, a bit of cloth from the children's hospital gown, a piece of your elegant gray dress and your school T-shirt—giving me an image of you that is within reach. Yet I am frightened, Éloïse. Will my body always remember your body? Will I always be able to replay your image, familiar and clear? Or will all these small details, which come to me so easily now, slowly fade, leaving me with clouded and fleeting memories of you?

I'm so afraid to lose this power of memory, so afraid that your hold over me might weaken. I know that this distancing will come in its time, driven by the obstinate and insistent force of the living. I will fight this abandonment with all my strength. I do not want your memory to lose its contours—to allow the past to uncouple and ultimately resign myself to a meaningless present. I don't have the courage to do it.

I caress the quilt of memory, touch the barrettes, the ribbons, a lock of your hair. Through them I revisit your lovely dreamy eyes, your gasping breath and unyielding spasticity. I've done my work well and I'm content with it. I need only to place the thermometer with your last temperature reading from a half-hour before you died, which still reads 109 degrees. I have cared for it preciously over all these months, as witness to your fever and the outrage of your broken body. It will go into its prepared place on Thursday the third of October, the anniversary of a first whole year without you.

Fourth Dream

You have just died. Revolted, your father wishes that there remain no trace of your past suffering. I tell him it's impossible, that whatever he does, there will always be something of your suffering in the memory of those who loved you. He cannot accept it. He takes you in his arms and carries you to the garage to crush your skull with a sledge. He wants no one to know that you existed with such pain. He is beyond reason. Beside myself, I want to go to the neighbors for help; out of control, he tries to stop me.

I wake up shivering.

My shivering wakes him up and I cry on his shoulder, unable to tell him my dream.

It is close to midnight. I nestle into your beanbag chair where we passed so many hours glued to each other, arms interlocked, your legs on mine, reading, talking, watching television or listening to music.

The passing on of your qualities has not been smooth. You had better know that your strength, which you flew as a banner in the heat of all our battles and that you passed on to me so I could continue in your place, let me down. It is becoming more and more remote. In many ways these last five days have been extremely trying. I fear I might start to crumble, that the fault lines in me will open into huge bottomless crevasses that I will slide into without resistance.

Your powerful will to live comes to me in waves, suddenly overpowering me and carrying me on majestic crests. It is then that I'm seized with urgency, and with complete awareness, taste eternity. But once the wave recedes, I am nothing but jetsam, incapable of moving.

Happily, I am more and more able to bring your tenderness into my life. If you only knew how sensitive I have become to everything that bears the softness of your hair or delicate neck. You probably know life's cruelties no longer make me cry, but every little random act of tenderness and caring is a glimpse of a soul. Yet I still throw myself into revolt with a scorching stubbornness—a flaming anger that burns everything in its path—but it soon gives way to a despondency that comes close to completely blotting me out. There are days when I crawl forward with my body so battered by contradictory emotions that I really have no idea what can save me. It's during such moments that a dangerous urge comes to me—to leave with no return ticket. I want to close myself in a fiery room, hear its cracking, feel its heat on my face and then finally go to sleep. The frontiers of the world would end at the doors of this isolated room. The fire would console me, dry my tears, calm my panic and reduce me to ashes.

The school bus, like an enormous yellow caterpillar with black antennae, always brightened up school days.

I see my blond one in his new shoes, his backpack, his multicolored snowsuit, run smiling across the street despite all my warnings to watch out when crossing.

And my curly brunette, when she was well enough to attend, left home in the morning with new ribbons in her hair, her just-about-to-talk mouth open, her bag hung on the wheelchair. She was swallowed up by the bus on her magic platform, content that she, like others, had her school bus too.

Early September. Back-to-school time. I went to work following the school route so I could slowly drive by the clusters of children and parents waiting for the bus.

Your brother, in all his normality, with a clear, predictable path. How he flooded me with such happiness! I remember the smell of his new notebooks before they took on the eccentric marks of their owner. Reminiscing, I felt the reassuring rhythm of those days whose gentle cadence swung between the leaving for and coming from school, vibrate in me.

You are very much on my mind this morning. The unending battles for your transportation to school come back to me as do the annual negotiations to have this service reinstated, the school integration issues, the countless committees and frustrations. I remember your happiness when you got to go school and your weariness when it was all too much; your daily diary we kept up with your teachers, and their patience, dedication and the concern they had for you and your schoolmates, evident by their many attempts to get through to you by over-stimulation.

I get to work all too soon and regret that I must start a new workday. A strange feeling is overpowering me.

A heavy door has closed completely, separating me from life.

The Nuthatch Nest

Her fascinated, beguiled, concentrated look when her father took her lovingly from tree to tree, like a bumble bee. Under each branch she seemed to distinguish a play of shadow and light between leaves and sunlight. What was it she saw then? What did she think?

Finally, a calm. I sit on the porch and savor a soft and vulnerable sun. Watching it set, I wonder if a sun sets and rises where you are. Have you discovered other miracles to replace our magnificent stars? True, your eyes could never contemplate the beauty of the world as I now see it.

In your memory, I close my eyes so I can no longer see the dusk—only feel it, like you did. My head back, my face offered to the last penetrating rays, I savor it deep in my soul. All is calm. My thoughts wander freely. I feel that I am set apart from my life, witnessing with detachment the years of energy, physical investment and emotional turbulence. All these years of love! The recent past, from which I hope to find some continuity, absorbs me intensely and colors the present with bold brush strokes. I am totally incapable of looking into the future, of organizing and orchestrating plans as I have done for the last forty years. I want only for it to come, to welcome it without provocation. I don't know what life is hiding behind its back, but I am not certain I really want to know, and I don't want to guess.

In the cold light of this Sunday morning, listening to Fauré's Requiem, I think of your liberated soul as the white inside-out flowers of the cyclamen.

If during all these years you could not escape from my enveloping love, on this October afternoon it seems to me that you have indeed escaped for good and have traveled into a dimension far beyond me. In letting you go, I have allowed you to pursue your destiny. All those years, you needed me as much as I needed you, and we both survived through the grace of this regenerating relationship. My love was your sustenance and your presence, my inspiration and motivation.

I cannot escape you through the all-encompassing nostalgia that slides me into your arms. And when I close my eyes, I feel your powerful gaze calling me with more force than all the voices of the world.

Libera me domine.

Fifth and final dream

You have been dead for some time.

I hide your cold body in a closet. Sometimes when I am alone, I take it in my arms. Each time I do, it becomes warm and alive. You come back. I gently rock you, happy to have found you for just a moment, to know you are there. I know, however, that what I'm doing should not be done, or at least, that no one should see me. But I continue to bring you back to life when I need to.

Again I open the closet, and again I take you in my arms and rock you. I am so happy. Then I suddenly realize your father and others are there watching me. They say nothing, but I know from their stares that I can't continue doing this. I tell them it's the last time and promise not to do it again. But before you leave, I want to convince them that your body comes to life each time I cradle it. I hug you and the miracle happens again. You're alive in my arms and your warmth spreads into me. I hug you as hard as I can. Sadly, I know it is the last time. The others have disappeared and we're alone— alone in the world. I close my eyes and hug you harder than ever, continue to rock, very gently, my little one

How good it is!

I awake crying, knowing that I have just said my farewell, my arms filled with a warmth that will stay with me for many more days.

In the deep of this November night I roam from room to room seeking haven. In the kitchen I press my forehead flat against the cold window pane, and watch a three-quarters moon dominate a clear, hard sky in which each star shines with its own brilliance, but none sends me any message. The pane reflects a tormented, conflicted image, "a tangle of matter and ghost" as Leonard Cohen once raucously sang with his beautiful voice.

When you were here I often placed my sleepless nights at your side. Incapable of sleep, I would stop by your room and find you awake, powerless even to turn on your side. I would lie down beside you, whisper my dreams to you, talk about my problems, tell you the stories of my day. You would breathe more quickly to let me know you knew I was there, to tell me you understood. I slipped a finger into your warm, stiff hand and then together we would wait till one or the other drifted into sleep. It wasn't always the same one, do you remember? Sometimes it was you; your breathing would become less labored and more regular, your hands would open up. Sometimes it was my turn, curled up, my head toward your shoulder, finally calmed—almost consoled.

Out of habit or need of consolation, I go to your room and write. This relieves my anguish. I would so much like to be able to have the power to recreate you with this string of words and images.

When the words don't come any longer, I contemplate the quilt. I look at it and think of you. I take the little golden scissors, feel their smooth surface on my palm and cut pieces from many your colored ribbons: mauve, golden, red. I thread them through my fingers, arrange them in rows on the floor, braid them, and finally, tired but breathing a little easier, I once more decide that I want to go on, and I go to bed.

I want to sleep, to abandon myself in unconsciousness and regenerate my soul, but sleep, this subterfuge for oblivion, slips away insidiously. Once again I am faced with the unacceptable—your absence. The year has just tipped towards its last half, and I sift through it reliving the first complete cycle without you. The first times—first week, first month, first springtime—are finished, forever. Tell me, how long can one go on measuring absence, counting emptiness, quantifying lack?

I know we have a tendency to do the same with happiness, celebrating anniversaries as though their very numbers were victories, but for loss? Tell me, why do we bother? Is it to prove to ourselves that we have survived the worst? Do I really have to measure my pain and count the days to know that my life will never continue with such gusto and innocence now that you have left me? I've had enough, Éloïse. I no longer want to stay rolled up, holding in my pain. I want to live, do you hear? I want to open my arms, lift up my head and laugh from deep in my gut. The air is soft and calls me to run in the fields. My time is rationed, let me enjoy it. Free me from this sadness, invest me with our shared love so that I can live each passing moment to the full.

Tell me, little grey chick, did I dream of these islands of peace in the midst of the day, these glimpses of a rare bird hidden in the heart of words and simple gestures? Did I dream the magic sap running in the forests, growing plants, breezes that linger, gestures which persist? Did I dream the stirring rhythm of my starved heart, colors that spring to life, the pulse of seasons?

It is not possible to speak of her passage amongst us without acknowledging with profound reverence the network of support, affection and love which she alone sustained.

Her aura affected all those who came near her. Devotion, patience, gentleness were woven into the web that surrounded her and grew with her over the years, expanding to include her family, her nanny, neighbors, friends and professionals, each one with a privileged place and function.

She returned a full measure to many by giving fuller meaning to their intervention, involvement, attachment and their love.

It is so dark. If I close my eyes, I'm rocked by deep torment, so I leave them open. And by taking deep breaths, I can stop myself from crying again.

It is so difficult without you; without your suffering to support, your sweetness to share or your strength to keep pace with. Throughout all these nights like tonight, my arms seek you out and I am lost inside the cage of my sadness.

I feel so used up. I want someone to rock me gently, singing "L'Eau Vive" as though I were little again.

I still cannot get used to the divide. Worse, it affects me more each day. I sulk, I shape the snow on your grave, I make snow angels, I cut ribbons, I sing songs in your memory, I hold your slipper to my heart. In short, I try to prolong you, to recreate you, to cause your rebirth.

When I behave myself, resigned to what everybody else except me has understood, I can see that too much of me has gone with you, that what remains can't surface. What remains is as vulnerable as the little girl who had so much difficulty breathing. What remains wants to go after you, follow you and ride the clouds to greet you.

Don't you see how badly I need a sign from you? Just some tiny signal: a half-smile from where you are, a whisper from the wings of the angel you have become, a brush on my cheek so I will know I am not alone anymore and I can find some confidence. Don't you see how I place myself in the way of any draft that could bring you to me any instant? Couldn't you visit your mother and for a brief moment invest her with your spirit?

In memory of your soft hair on my cheek,
of your head resting against my shoulder,
of sloppy and joyful kisses on my mouth,
of your hand resting in mine.

Éloïse, is there another address where I can reach you?

Do you see me?

I snuggle in bed, drinking coffee, absorbing the grayness of this last March day. Even now, there is a hollowed place at my side, just for you. From my pillows I can see the nuthatch nest, signaling the mysteries of life from between the languid yellow branches of the willow. What calmness and silence! My body is the image of this hibernating earth, deep down alive with the pungent underwood, full of sighs and crackles. Of course, you already know how much your mother is a woman of springtime, full of impetuosity, ready to be carried by the mysteries and passions of life. Perhaps you would like to suggest that in getting older she should seek out a greater serenity, a supple wisdom, a late-afternoon peace? Tell me, how can I ignore this part of me that does not wish to be tamed, that feeds on intensity and absolutes, this dimension of my soul that needs the flood waters?

Battles rage inside me. Borders are no longer as well defined as before and I feel the need to change my alliances. These internal wars drain and distract me. I no longer know how to broker peace with myself or those I love.

To stall for time I begin my own dance of spring, a ballet for two arms only. I turn the soil in the garden, adding compost, ashes and fertilizer. My back and arms are stronger than I thought. The colors are a wonder of many shades of brown. Despite its cold layers, the earth is pierced. I throw myself into this work with gusto and gradually I give way to a delicious tiredness.

In a pale blue sky a watery, waning moon brings on a timid peace, an apparent truce. I try to listen for the birds rather than the drumming of my soul. But it would take the turning of a hundred gardens to wear out this impetuous spirit that has wind in its sails and will never find calm seas.

In cedar, at the front and back of the house, the access ramps made for her wheelchair are still there, ready for her.

And in the kitchen cupboard, on the right shelf, there is an emptiness where her medication used to be.

I miss the daily routine of repetitive acts of love and tenderness performed for you and for my family of past, full days. How is it kind gestures never wear down through time or repetition? I fear that I didn't appreciate you enough during the time we shared.

If only we knew before death what we become aware of after—is it the finality of it that gives what we already know the force of blows?

You were always my refuge from storms, despair and fright. You received me in the bent angles of your body and enveloped me in your unthinkable softness. Exhausted, I nestled in your sweet-smelling hair; in the hollow of your palm, which I would open up like an oyster hiding a precious pearl; or in your body, wrapped around mine like a Chinese puzzle.

Now lost and separated by an infinite universe, I turn into myself, wearing away the strands of my memory. How difficult it is to tame these new emotional dimensions I must learn to cope with—they are so completely opposed to my known world.

Tell me, can one truly be consoled by something one can't touch, taste or see? How much I want to imagine you real in a celestial home, a place of familiar textures, colors and smells. I want to be able to say that, yes, finally you are complete, happy to be free. But my own freedom is too heavy for me and my back bows under the weight of the unknown. Perhaps, seeing me in this state, you are as troubled as I am and unable to continue your transformation.

I would like to find you someday, where you would be my mother and I your daughter. Would I have the courage to be the severely injured daughter, the ruined little girl, dependent on others for all her needs?

Because she could not sit up without a brace, I had to lower the passenger seat when she rode with me in the car. How many times did we drive home from the clinic, holding hands and almost always crying because of some new pronouncement of something we already knew. Significant deterioration; erosion of her quality of life; hope turned back once more.

There is one ritual I cannot abandon, it is the return home after work, a sort of spiritual re-enactment that falsely preserves me from reality. Even now, two years after the fracturing of my family, I still arrive home, breathless, hoping to find my demanding children. I open the door lightheartedly and then—if you only knew how dark and empty this house can be, a ghost ship stranded in a sea of obsessive silence. What other place could I go to that would be as good as that sanctuary in time where you all waited for me at the end of the day? Perpetuating habit, I swing the door open and wander around this emptiness. I stubbornly continue to imagine open arms and faces, but each time, it's the same deception. Often, when I am completely paralyzed in front of the mute windows, incapable of opening the door, I turn around and drive through the hills. I take my pain for a ride, a tour of the trees, bare or full depending on the seasons. I am soothed by the sound of the motor so I rarely leave the car; it protects, encapsulates, detaches me from the world. In its moving carapace I feel secure.

These wanderings, however somber they may be, are nothing compared to my nocturnal escapades. When I run away at night, anguish, shattering in a thousand sharp shards, makes me lose control, readies me to be swept away forever. I often must stop at the roadside, my heart racing, eyes blinded by tears, fearful of this endless road that seems to go nowhere. I beat on the wheel, crying out my pain, repeating the same pleas, afraid I will never be able to stop crying. A few hours later when I robotically return home, I feel neither soothed nor consoled—I simply feel exhausted, broken, empty, usually for many days. I do this sad wandering in the backwoods of life in secret.

My afternoon jaunts, however, lead me more calmly along the sinewy roads, each turn slowly reducing my impatience. The fields of wild grasses pass by, the tired shoulders of the mountains contain me in their timeless arms, fence posts secure frontiers and the proud and independent presence of the trees set me an example. Never having the courage to break with everything, I invariably meet up with the road home and prudently renegotiate reality. I enter the house furtively, turn on as few lights as possible, and in the dusky light, I go about the day-to-day chores, now so hard to accomplish.

Then your father comes home. My companion, ally and witness. I steal a glance at him and realize that we are now alone, enclosed in our individual and shared mourning, endowed with a vulnerable, yet precious life, with an intimacy which needs to be redefined. The day you died, Éloïse, we both lost our particular status. From the invincible team we made up for so many years we have become two solitary beings, facing each other, completely stripped down. In leaving, you took away our privileged role of protectors of our little girl, our very special child. For thirteen years, day and night, the moral and physical support for each other was unwavering. Thirteen years is a long time. With our heads bowed towards the tempest, we were united in a deep and marvelous alliance—incorruptible, loyal, understanding and creative. But once you left, we had to revise our roles: two individuals isolated by a grief, too keen to be shared, dizzy on the edge of emptiness. So we continue, silently, often side by side, sometimes enemies. Each day it becomes apparent that our first reconciliation must happen inside; that each of us must find a new identity before beginning a new shared life. Perhaps it is only when each one of us is able to survive on their own, to breathe by themselves, that we will then be reunited in a reinvented harmony, strengthened by the past, which instead of destroying us, will make us so much stronger.

There is your brother Nicolas. Not only has he been deprived of his childhood accomplice and his most fervent admirer, but he has also inherited the heavy solitude of being the survivor, now an only child invested with all the dreams of his parents. He lived through your death in his full adolescence, at an age when he thought he was invincible. I so much wished to have spared him this premature confrontation with death. I now see him, so handsome with his long hair, sharp eyes rich with the future. He wears one of your earrings in his left ear while I wear the other. My heart overflows with love for him to the point of breathlessness.

I beg you, watch over him.

Always, she is standing by my side
She's my inspiration and she's my battle cry
And in her arms is the only place I know
Where peaceful waters flow.

—Chris de Burgh, "Where Peaceful Waters Flow"

It has been two years since our paths separated, since you took your leave as delicately as you could. One by one you undid the chains which held you prisoner; the ones that weighed down your breathing, curled and deformed your body, brought down a dark veil over your eyes and prevented you from forming much awaited words.

I now have to admit it, there was one word above all, on the tip of your tongue, so close to spilling out but impossible for you to articulate; one word I waited for, looked for, hoped for in every movement of your mouth and with each one of your prolonged sighs. One word that would have rekindled all my energy, prepared me for all battles, allowed me to move mountains and carry you in triumph on my shoulders. Just one word dear girl, *Mama*.

No child has ever pronounced this simple noun with such love and fervor as you did, in your silence. In your expert way you always knew how to call to me; imperiously, yet with tenderness, you summoned me not only to your side, but to your rages and your bleakness too. Hand in hand, hearts entwined, we slowly advanced together towards the final rupture.

Stubborn as only I can be, I am still waiting for this word. I'm watching for it in the wind rustling the leaves, in a far-off cry during a sleepless night, in the indiscriminate noise of everything that is still alive.

Éloïse, please listen to me carefully: I will always be your mother, but tell me how I can remain if there is no longer anything I can do for you except let you go? Is this really the final, impossible trial? Let you go? Take a deep breath, open all the doors and windows of the soul and say go, my dear one, you can; soar like a magnificent bird for you are finally released.

Somehow I always thought I was ready to take on anything for you, with you. But you see, I didn't foresee the powerful selfishness that now, deep within, possesses me to keep you in a locked room from which I can't and won't let you escape.

Before your death, when faced with your often intolerable suffering, there were concrete acts I could perform to support you, to ease and to share in your incomprehensible destiny. You needed me.

My dearest, broken little girl, do you know how many times I rehearsed your death? I really thought I could prepare myself to accept it more easily once it happened. In my mind's eye I made you die, and each time, believed it. Tears flowed and I truly thought I was on the road to acceptance. But however often I made you die in my head, I never let you leave my heart, and all these rehearsals were, in the end, quite useless.

On the day of your death, you forced me into a room where there was no one to guide me. Since that day, it's as though I am waking from a dream without ever having been asleep. As if everything that was solid and firm for years suddenly dissolved into a complex fluidity, leaving me in flux, unable to find solid ground, madly reaching for the clouds.

At the crematorium, they said it would be very quick—she was so small. We waited for her ashes in an adjoining room, pacing back and forth, sadly thinking of what her body was becoming.

After a half hour, I glanced through the porthole window exactly at the same time as the oven was opened. The left side of her skull and her ribcage were still intact, glowing red. To the very end, she affirmed herself with force, determination, courage, in all her beauty.

I am cold everywhere. I want you to take me in your arms as I took you in mine. I want you to run your long hand in my dull and graying hair and rest your forehead against my stomach, all the while rocking with me, for a long, long time.

I am so cold in this early November morning, in this unending darkness. Tell me how to reuse the two wrecks that my arms have become, how to fill this gapping hole that stops me from breathing.

I am cold because of your absence. You engaged all my senses: hearing your breathing, smelling your fragrance early in the morning, touching all the hard angles of your mangled body, tasting your clear sweet saliva on my moistened lips, seeing you, Éloïse; and in seeing you, believing in you.

I am cold from remaining stalled with my suffering and confusion from our broken attachment. In this world, with its mutable values, I want you to know that nothing will ever replace what we lived through. It is a state of grace for the survivor to savor the memory of the other with tenderness.

Finally, I am cold from the desire to join you where your magic has left a smattering of stars.

My dear one,

Everything we've lived through should make me stronger. Our shared battles, your injuries, the false prognosis, the prejudices, and above all, the wearing down represent too much conquered ground to allow me to abandon the field. I must create a new strength by combining what remains of mine with the legacy of yours.

Strength, this arduous discipline, never attainable but always within reach, must be retrieved with will—as if such a state of grace could exist on its own.

Strength, the armor preserving us both, within which a powerful and unwavering love bloomed.

Saturday and Sunday mornings our bed became a play-ground when we shared coffee. I gave it to her and she dribbled it everywhere in pleasure.

That would be her last taste of life when she could no longer take anything else: two fingers in the cup, then onto her tongue, cup then tongue, cup to tongue until the point when even those drops were too much.

You know, there is a new warmth growing in me. Slowly, softly, darkness is displaced by openness—a space where it is possible to breathe freely and soar with my wings. A larger, freer space where I can feel you at my side, even though I can no longer pull on the umbilical cord which always attached me to you. Nothing physically attaches us anymore, Éloïse, nothing at all. Our bodies have become mere accessories, distant and separate for eternity. Having been fused together so long, I know that I will always suffer from this terrible amputation. Perhaps I am now ready to tell you, "Go, loved one, I allow you to leave, you may take flight."

I must finally see the evidence that our wonderful physical relationship is over. If my arms mourn you, they also keep in them the vibrant richness of your passage and the indestructible memory of having held you in such a short, yet intense, embrace.

To know love—to be invested by it with all one's being—is a rare and precious gift. Not everyone can love with such intensity, because there is a price to pay, obligations arising from the investiture of such power.

Nowhere is this love so evident as in absence and all its aspects. First, the little departures, like unforeseen surprises that slip into a day and relentlessly chip away at you. Then comes the gradual pulling away from what you believed to be eternal, these small, insistent withdrawals imposed one on the other: spaces between telephone calls, loss of concentration never to be found again. Finally comes the great rift when the other leaves, forever. In the end, someone always leaves, someone goes away; never to return. The road parts, the other leaves and won't be there tomorrow. The void left by departure is in equilibrium with the intensity of sharing before the separation, followed by the unbearable ripping away.

Éloïse, I want you to know that nothing in this world will make me regret loving you as much as I did, as much as I forever will. In return I have received your undivided devotion, even if I must now live with the aftermath of your death. The strength of love which dwelled in us continues to give my life richness, texture and hope.

PARALYZED

You made me move
to the rhythms of seasons,
fluid cadence of feelings.
Dance has come to me,
music floods my arms, my legs
and dried womb.
You beat your wings,
send me breathlessly running
further than despair,
as fast as life's dreams.

BLIND

You opened my eyes
to the glistening colors,
smooth forms of all that moves around me,
fireworks of nature,
the firm contours of a hand
extended in the night of desire.
The nuances of a look that lingers,
the irresistible light of a smile,
the gentleness of tears.

MUTE

You left me with words to mourn you,
writing to you across the universe.
Silent words, whispered words,
notes, letters, smothered cries,
forlorn, without end.
Unending ribbons, bright as our love.
I attach them to my heart and make bows
of words never said,
a thousand times repeated,
thrown by hazard to your planets.

OPPRESSED

You gave me long and melodious sighs,
profound breaths, swelled with air,
love and tenderness.
Alive with a new spring lightness
my lungs pump a new blood
that gives life to the branches
of my body.
I inhale—I exhale
precious urgency of living
present already passed.

Dead

You spun me out in all directions.
North of my hurt
where you looked out for me.
South of an aggressive life
at the discovery of new continents.
East of Eden and its quests
insatiable hunger, lust for rebirth.
West of an everyday life,
cocooned continuity
forgotten tenderness.

Resurrected

You fixed me in my mortality,
which devours the present
and invites me over the edge.
Thanks to you, I know more than ever
that today is my last chance
to encompass life with energy
to the limits of a leading heart,
wounded but stronger soul
and this body, mine,
so wondrously incarnate.

The Blackbird's Song

My sweetest girl,

I want to tell you that I not only nourished, cared for and held you through all these years, but in so doing, I also nourished, cared for and held myself. I loved you before you learned to love me, I was sick when you were sick, I suffered when you suffered—and long afterward as well. My flesh didn't die with yours the afternoon you went, but a part of my soul came apart, separated from me and followed you into death. It was a part of me that was yours completely and will belong to you forever. In the same way, a part of you remains in my soul, like an island adrift and floating in the current of time, leaving silence in its wake. I am comforted to know that through its presence, the part of me that is you will be forever disconsolate.

Even though I can laugh and love again, I still miss you. I still have the desire to be with you, sometimes it is biting, sometimes it is softly nostalgic. They say something dies in you when you live through the unlivable; but you know, we eventually come to accept the unacceptable. In doing so, I have lost my innocence, yet at the same time my heart is now open to a new world. I know that an unfathomable sadness will lurk inside each happiness, in the core of all my passions. In this rush of reconciliation, I also realize that our love is now invulnerable to change. Wherever you are, my Éloïse, without form or bonds, well beyond anything I could have wished for you and certainly you are well above what you would have been had you remained with us.

Your departure also allowed me to look into myself, to listen more attentively to my inner voice. I am now learning to be alone and to have confidence. I want to see with my own light, to let things come to me unbidden.

The learning has just begun.

For the third time since your departure, spring brings its arrival. The season hides, snuggled up under the snow, and then will explode across the land.

> Impatient trees
> freed streams
> loosened buds
> adventurous roots
> blood in the veins
> unsated desire...

The whole earth is in me, ready to warm up. Softly, insistently, the sun caresses my forehead. Just like you, color comes back to me in cheerful freckles and my heart beats faster.

It is the endurance of cycles.

I close my eyes and concentrate on the long roots that begin to grow deep within my soul. I, too, am getting ready to blossom again.

I open curious eyes again,
generous arms, soft hands,
thirsty heart.
I breathe deeply and listen
to the life around me,
at once so strong, yet vulnerable.

Melting snow, falling ice,
red-wings on a branch,
shouts of children at play,
tumult of my heart,
silence of my hurt.

The two of us, my love, are on the edge of a big, oval, yellow nest,
hand in hand,
glorious,
at the crossroads of worlds.

I turn and look towards you...
How can you still be so beautiful?

Softly, I caress you with all my love,
then I release my fingers.

We smile at each other

and I hear

the sound of my own voice whispering

the sound of my own voice whispering

the sound of my own voice whispering

Yes, Éloïse.

Swan Song

A picture of Tracy and her father taken when her pain was still bearable. Smiling, she is anchored in her father's arms while he holds her—strength mingled with tenderness.

We hear of their tragedy on the news, we read about it in the papers, but always return to this picture for warmth, for understanding, for comfort.

Love and trust both ways, until the end.

A Letter to Tracy Latimer

$\mathcal{T}$racy, dear soul,

We have never met, so I hope you will accept my need to speak out to you.

Like my Éloïse, your damaged brain condemned you to a life of dependency. Severe quadriplegic cerebral palsy left you incapable of any voluntary movement. You were unable to move your legs, arms or head, unable to talk or chew, blind to the beauty of the world and the loving faces of those who cared for you, subject to massive uncontrollable seizures, and as if all this were not enough, an unknown degree of mental retardation.

I am sorry if it is painful for you to hear all this again, but I must go on so that it's clearly understood what you and your parents lived with for thirteen long years.

Put in a drug-induced coma in your early days to reduce the swelling of your brain, you endured a myriad of tests and insults to your tiny body: spinal taps, brain scans, electroencephalograms. For years, you were subjected to a never-ending schedule of interventions that did nothing to commute the merciless sentence gravity was imposing on your body.

You could not be cured.

Nonetheless, radical surgical procedures were performed to alleviate symptoms: cutting the abductor muscles in your legs and the cords in your heel to redistribute strain and relieve pressure on your hip; putting your body in a cast from armpits to toes so you could heal properly; wiring two steel rods to your spine and bolting them to your pelvis (an eight-hour operation with nothing but Tylenol to relieve your pain after the procedure) because the irreversible scoliosis, a severe curvature of the spine, was crushing your lungs and depleting you of oxygen.

Your poor besieged body, my love: muscle tension and atrophy, dislocated hips, bronchial infections, daily seizures, constant vomiting, plugged bowels, prostheses of all kinds. And through these ordeals, your uncomprehending self was unable to verbalize its volition or signal its revolt. How could you endure so much? How could your parents? Helplessly and with diminishing hope, they witnessed the inevitable deterioration of your body with no relief in sight, a continuous decline in the quality of your life and an ever-increasing quotient of pain.

You knew Tracy, as did your parents, that you were not disabled, but severely injured. You were not handicapped, but permanently dependant on others for all your needs. You did not have special needs, you were totally needy.

But your parents loved you so, their vulnerable, yet strong little girl, gentle, yet brave big girl; a daughter who was dependent, yet a source of inspiration for all, with a radiant sixth sense emanating from your very soul. Your soul provided them with a light that kept them going day after day, until that light started to fade, when all that was left was the endless suffering of your daily agony.

You must know how much you meant to your family, in the same way Éloïse meant so much to us. They could never relinquish their need to protect and care for you—and they did so, in their way, to the very end.

Tracy, have you and Éloïse wondered why you inherited such a life?

Please, please tell me you are happier now.

Let me imagine both of you running hand in hand across the unknown, moving, seeing, talking, singing, thankful for liberation, free of pain.